WE ARE THE

WEIRD ONES

EMBRACE YOUR WEIRD

FOR A KINDER,

MORE INCLUSIVE WORLD

MALLORY WHITFIELD

MISS
MALAPROP
PRESS

Mallory Whitfield / Miss Malaprop Press
New Orleans, Louisiana

QUANTITY PURCHASES:

Miss Malaprop Press is pleased to offer most books at a discount when purchased in quantity. Professional groups, companies, and other organizations may qualify for special terms when ordering this title. For more information, please email hello@mallorywhitfield.com.

We Are The Weird Ones: Embrace Your Weird for a Kinder, More Inclusive World,

Mallory Whitfield. —1st ed.

ISBN 979-8-9852754-0-7

In loving memory of Vee.

May we all tackle life so ferociously.

TABLE OF CONTENTS

ACTION

We Are The Weird Ones

Have you ever felt left out? Like you didn't belong? Have you ever felt... weird?

I think at some point most of us have felt weird, felt like an outsider, or like we didn't belong. I know I did. Growing up, I always felt weird. I was even called "weird." And sure, I had friends, but I didn't always feel like I *belonged*. I still feel this way as an adult sometimes, even among groups of friends.

What I've realized is, at some point in our lives, almost everybody feels this way. To feel "weird" is pretty normal. I realized that as humans, we're all weird *and* we're all normal. We're both, at the same time. It's one of the things that makes being human so hard *and* so amazing. Each one of us has certain experiences that are unique to us, but we're all human beings. We are all special, shiny snowflakes *and* we are boring, ordinary people. Being human is complex.

Each of us has things that we share in common with pretty much everyone else. We need food, water, and clean air to survive, of course. But our human needs go deeper than that. We all want to feel loved. We all want to belong. And when we help other people feel like they belong, it can make *us* feel like *we* belong, too.

So often, our fears of not belonging are also fears of being judged. But what if we stopped judging ourselves and others so harshly? What if we stopped judging other people's "weird" like it's a bad thing, and instead we celebrated all of the beautifully weird things about ourselves and others? What if we stopped judging what's "normal" as if there's a single, correct answer for what "normal" is?

The idea of "normal" is weird to me. For example, if having a "normal family" means having a family with no dysfunction, addiction, abuse, or mental illness whatsoever... a family where everyone gets along all the time... I don't think I know anyone who has a normal family. And if you DO have a normal family by that definition, then count yourself lucky, because your family is pretty weird compared to most people's experiences.

We judge other people who are different from us as "weird" because we have this ridiculous idea that "normal" exists as one singular definition. But it doesn't! Each one of us has our own lived experiences that shape our idea of what "normal" means to us. What's "normal" for someone who grew up on the Mississippi Gulf Coast, like I did, is probably very different from what's "normal" for someone who grew up in New York City or Paris, France. All sorts of things shape our individual definition of "normal." We are influenced by the opinions and values of the people who raised us. We're influenced by the culture we grow up in, whether that's on a global, national, or local scale. We're influenced by the circumstances of our upbringing. What's "normal" for someone who grew up in a wealthy family is very different from what is "normal" for someone who experienced hunger or homelessness as a child.

People often use the label "weird" as a way to judge people who are different from them. But I don't believe that being weird is bad. Our **weird** is our strength. Our weird is that magic spark that makes us who we are. It's our individuality. It's our unique combination of life experiences, memories, strengths, gifts, and talents that only we have.

If we want to build a kinder, more inclusive world where everyone feels like they belong, the path towards together lies in embracing our own **weird** — our differences — so we can also embrace what is different about other people.

Okay, but maybe you're wondering.... "How? How do I embrace my weird? How do I stop judging myself and others because of our differences?"

I won't lie. It isn't always easy. It takes practice — a lifetime of it. But there are four key things I try to remember and put into practice any time those judgments creep up. I'd like to introduce you to something I call the **Wheel of Weird**:

WHEEL OF WEIRD

curiosity | compassion

authenticity | action

The Wheel of Weird is a framework — a way of remembering the ways we can embrace our differences as well as the differences of others. The Wheel of Weird is about looking inward at the judgments we have about ourselves, and it's also about looking outward at the judgments we make about other people.

The four parts of the Wheel of Weird are **Curiosity**, **Compassion**, **Authenticity**, and **Action**.

WHEEL OF WEIRD

curiosity

Born Curious

I was always a naturally curious kid, as most children are. While I did well in school, my hunger for learning and knowledge went far beyond the classroom. I was experimental and expressive in some settings, and shy and introverted in others. (I still am!) These dual sides of my personality, mixed with my interest in things outside of the norm meant I was *definitely* called weird as a kid.

Around middle school, I hit my peak as the weird kid. Middle school is awkward for most of us, but my adolescent obsession with actor Jeff Goldblum made me extra eccentric. I remember seeing *Jurassic Park* when it came out in theaters in 1993, and from then on, I was smitten. At one point, I was so in love that I created a hand-written catalog on a piece of notebook paper based on an Internet Movie Database list of all of his movies and characters. I used color-coded stars to make note of if I had seen that movie and if I owned that movie on VHS videotape. Then, I marked, "What would my relationship be with his character in that movie?" Would I be friends with his character? Would I date his character? Would I marry his character? Would I make love to his character?

When I was in eighth grade, I printed out a picture of his character from the 1986 sci-fi horror classic *The Fly*. In case you haven't seen the movie, the premise is that Jeff Goldblum is a nerdy scientist who is trying to build a teleportation device. The whole thing goes haywire and he accidentally splices his genetic material with a housefly and turns into a fly monster. But before that happens, there's a famous scene where he's testing the teleportation device and for some reason, he needs to be naked to test it. His legs are strategically placed so you never see his dangly bits, but still... the guy is naked. Somehow, I thought it was a good idea to bring this picture to school with me one day. I was showing it to my best friend when my teacher caught me. She said, "Mallory. You cannot have this picture. This photo of Jeff Goldblum is pornography, which you cannot have in the eighth-grade classroom." Oops!

At the time, my choice of middle school crush was a strange one, but these days it's practically trendy to think of the quirky actor as a sex symbol. (Just check out some of the comments on Jeff Goldblum's Instagram posts to see what I mean.)

Isn't it funny how a lot of the things that we get teased about as kids end up being pretty "normal" or common as adults? Another thing I was interested in as a teenager, which seemed a bit out of the ordinary back then but is pretty common now, was dying my hair blue. My mom was supportive of the idea, but my dad, a pretty conservative guy raised in southern Mississippi, warned me, "Gal, if ya dye your hair blue, people will judge you."

I'm sure my eyes almost rolled backward out of my head at the time, but as I got older I looked back on that and realized he had a point. If I dyed my hair blue, it would be a litmus test. Certain people *would* judge me negatively, even think of me as "weird" for having blue hair, while other people would judge me *positively* for the exact same thing.

It got me thinking about the other types of judgments that people make. We make judgments all the time about each other. Some are positive judgments, while others are negative. Some are judgments we realize that we're making, while others are unconscious judgments. As members of society, each one of us has unconscious biases and beliefs that come from the culture in which we were raised. People judge each other based on their hair color, skin color, weight, height, what kind of clothes you wear, where you grew up, what type of job you have, the type of people you hang out with.... People make judgments all the time about other people. And it makes me wonder, *why* do people make these judgments?

As I got more and more curious about this, I began to imagine the way that the world must have been a long, long time ago. If you think back to tens of thousands of years ago when we lived in much smaller societies, these judgments that we make about people we don't know might have helped us survive. In a world where we lived in tiny towns or small tribes of people, we might only know the same 100 or 200 people our entire lives. If someone new or different entered our lives, and they didn't look or sound like us, they could have been a threat. So judging other people who were different from us could have kept us safe.

But today we live in a much different world. Now, with the increasing pace of technology, we come in contact with all sorts of people from around the world all the time. We live in a magical time where we can meet, work with, become friends with, and even fall in love with people who are very different from us. We can connect with people who not only look different from us but people who were raised very differently from us. People whose definition of "normal" is different than ours. We get to learn *from* each other and *with* each other if we're willing to be curious about each other's differences.

"You Don't Sound Like … "

How might we remember our shared humanity? How might we be more curious about others, and about ourselves? If we had more conversations — more real, open, honest, vulnerable conversations — what could we gain?

There's so much fascinating stuff we can learn about other people and ourselves when we start with a willingness to be curious instead of coming from a place of judgment when topics get uncomfortable. Here's an uncomfortable thing I noticed about myself, that I started getting curious about:

I grew up on the Mississippi Gulf Coast. When people find that out, I often get asked about my lack of a Southern accent. I've been asked this question enough, it's made me wonder, "Why don't I have a Southern accent?"

I did a lot of theater growing up, so I wondered if that was part of it. Maybe by learning how to speak with a British accent or pretending to be other characters, I'd made my own accent more neutral?

But then I started thinking that there might be a subconscious part of me that had a stigma against the Southern accent and what it represents to a lot of people. I understood from a young age the way that a lot of people judge other people who have strong Southern accents. If you look at movies and popular culture, people with Southern accents are often portrayed as stupid, backward, or racist. So maybe I unconsciously trained myself to have a more neutral way of speaking to distance myself from that.

As I've grown older, however, I've tried to embrace what it means to be Southern. Despite our dark history, there are a lot of beautiful, amazing things about the whole southeastern United States. We've got delicious Southern food and plenty of beautiful scenery. Despite being some of the poorest states in the nation, the South is rich in arts and culture. This region has produced some of the most celebrated American writers, playwrights, and musicians, not to mention being the birthplace of jazz, blues, and rock and roll.

A few years ago, I was delighted to discover a website called The Bitter Southerner. Founded in 2013 and headquartered in Atlanta, Georgia, this digital publication was created to shatter stereotypes and challenge misconceptions about what it means to be Southern. In 2018, Time magazine named co-founder Chuck Reece among "31 People Who Are Changing the South." When describing The Bitter Southerner's community of readers, writers, and contributors, Reece called it "a community of anyone who's ever felt like a misfit in the South." *I feel so seen.* Via in-depth stories, photo essays, and podcasts, The Bitter Southerner tackles topics ranging from the cultural significance of Waffle House to Nashville's homeless community, to Houston's hip-hop scene, to decades-old community hubs in the Mississippi Delta, to Southern coastal towns on the brink of vanishing from climate change. They even have articles and a whole podcast episode about the very thing I was curious about: the judgments that folks have about the Southern accent. (Plus the folks who have made it their life's mission to preserve the dialects that are spoken across the South.)

Y'all, I love that journalists are doing this kind of work. People who are reflecting on the problematic parts of our past and present, as well as exploring the beauty of our individual subcultures. And hey, the word "y'all"? That's as inclusive as it gets! It just might be the best gender-neutral plural pronoun ever!

Wherever we come from, what can we learn from understanding and acknowledging the uncomfortable parts of our history? If we don't acknowledge the uncomfortable parts of our history, how can we grow from them and move past them?

I try to be more mindful now since I had this realization about my own judgments about the Southern accent and what it represents. For the same reasons I trained the accent out of myself, I've had plenty of times where if somebody else had a strong Southern accent, I had an aversion to it. Now, if I hear a strong Southern accent — or any accent — I try to notice it and say, "Okay, Mallory, why are you having this reaction?" and then listen to the person and the content of what they're saying, rather than the *way* they're saying it. Can I judge them based on the conversations we have together rather than something as superficial as the way they sound?

I'm working to be more mindful of this, but I'm not perfect. None of us are. We're all human. We all have unconscious bias and we all make judgments about other people. There are still plenty of people that when I first meet them, for whatever reason, get on my nerves or rub me the wrong way. But what I've been trying to do more recently, instead of making snap judgments about them, is to get curious and wonder, "Why don't I like this person? Why is my initial instinct to be annoyed or be put off?"

If we can approach someone else's differences — their "weird" — with a curiosity about, "Why did they come to believe something opposite of my belief?" instead of coming to it with a judgment like, "I'm right and you're wrong, therefore, we have nothing in common, we can't get along..." When we approach them with curiosity, it can create a bridge between the two people.

Getting Curious About Curiosity

I once heard Elizabeth Gilbert (author of *Eat, Pray, Love* and *Big Magic*) remark on a podcast interview that the opposite of depression is not happiness — it's curiosity. Happiness is fleeting, and it's hard to nail down exactly what it means to be happy. When people tell you to be happy or cheer up, *how* do you do so? If you think about "to be happy" as a verb... What does that really mean, anyway? On the other hand, to "be curious" is much more tangible and actionable.

As I discussed this concept with my therapist, we noticed how curiosity is also the opposite of fear. When you are actively curious about something or someone — when you're in the middle of exploration, asking questions, and seeking to understand — at least in those brief moments, fear and sadness hit the snooze button. It's hard for those emotions to exist simultaneously with curiosity. They may come back once curiosity has passed, but for those brief moments of curious questioning, it's hard for the darkest emotions to exist.

Curiosity brings about openness and playfulness. In many ways, society has trained us not to be curious. A school system based on tests and rules teaches rote memorization. It doesn't always encourage true learning and knowledge seeking. From childhood, we are often punished when we question authority. As children, we are sometimes punished for asking "why" questions at all. Parents and teachers often become exhausted by the curious ways of children. But we are *born* curious. Our natural desire is to seek out our own truth and pull back the onion layers of existence. For many of us, as we grow older, society pushes us to quiet this desire. It stamps out the fire of our curiosity. But some of us rebel. We embrace curiosity anyway. Society cannot break all of us from the desire for truth and understanding, for learning.

Although I always made good grades and excelled at school in many ways, I never felt like I was learning the full truth. Adults told us *what* to think. Being taught *how* to think — how to learn, ask questions, and seek truth — was much rarer.

I was lucky to have a few rebels in my life: other folks who weren't content with the status quo answers provided by traditional schooling or society. And I was lucky to have parents who let me leave high school early, halfway through my junior year when the "what" I was being forced to learn didn't meet my needs for understanding the actual workings of the world. Around the time I left high school, I remember reading *Lies My Teacher Told Me: Everything Your American History Textbook Got Wrong* by James W. Loewen. It examines the system of textbook publishing in the United States and how certain places with large school districts — like the state of Texas, for example — play a key role in determining which version of history children all across the country were taught. That book offered one of my first eye-opening lessons on the ways that I'd been duped. I realized not only that history is typically written by the victors (aka, a very narrow demographic of people throughout human existence), but also how much influence and control a few people with money and power can have over the children of an entire nation.

After dropping out of high school early, I got my GED, then attended community college for a year, and finally graduated from Loyola University New Orleans with a bachelor's degree in history. In college, I began to explore more of the stories of people I hadn't learned much about when I was younger. There was the rise of the Nazis and a German population left impoverished and fearful after World War I who were easily manipulated by the promises of a charismatic leader named Adolf Hitler. There were the vast and complex histories of India and Africa. During those classes, my heart sank as I learned more about the devastating effects of European colonialism. As part of my studies, I wrote research papers on everything from the first-wave feminists of England in the early 20th century, to gay subculture in New York City in the late 19th and early 20th centuries, to how Romani women from eastern Europe were traditionally sent to segregated living quarters during menstruation. My understanding of human history barely scratches the surface of its true depth. As I immersed myself in the stories and experiences of people from far beyond my own background, however, I began to understand and empathize with both the beauty and tragedy of human existence.

Now, as globalization and technology bring us closer together than ever before, it is important to me to stay curious. To continue to seek understanding. I shy away when someone calls me an "expert" — about anything, even topics I may be very knowledgeable about. To me, the word "expert" sounds like someone who knows everything about a subject. But humanity, with its diverse range of cultures and experiences, feels far too vast for any one of us to be an absolute expert on. We can each be experts on our own lived human experiences. And we can be seekers in understanding the experiences of others. A "curious seeker" is what I would rather be called and what I try to mindfully take action on. To stay curious and continue to seek understanding isn't always easy. Having curious conversations with others can be uncomfortable and even painful. It often requires us to re-examine our own biases, ways of doing things, and our pre-existing understanding of the world. To change your opinions about something, to leave behind what you once thought to be true... that can feel like a little part of you has died. And yet, sometimes it is only after one thing passes that there is room for something new and greater to be born.

My Normal, or Yours?

"Normal" is subjective. The more curious I get about experiencing things from another person's perspective, the more I appreciate this.

Living in New Orleans, I've realized what passes for "normal" here would probably be pretty weird in Cincinnati, for instance. Here, I hang out with drag queens, burlesque dancers, and bartenders. For New Orleanians, seeing someone in a ridiculous costume in public on any given day of the week is perfectly normal.

Around the world, the places we live shape our ideas about what is normal and what is weird. When we can travel, we can experience this firsthand. What is normal for me is probably very different for someone who grew up in Tokyo. I went to Japan for the first time a few years ago. Back home, I may look pretty normal, but in Japan, I was suddenly in the minority. I don't speak Japanese. But through the magic of Google Translate, I got to experience a taste of a different version of "normal." I met and had conversations with people who, once we started talking, I had a lot in common with. I quickly felt a kinship with people I'd just met, as we started to discuss *Star Wars* or a mutual background in the performing arts.

I had a similar experience at home in New Orleans when I attended an event at the New Orleans Deaf Church. Much like I had barely any knowledge of Japanese before going to Japan, I had barely any knowledge of American Sign Language before attending this event, where speaking was not allowed. Once again, I was in the minority. I was out of my depth. I was in a world where my version of "normal" — being able to hear — was abnormal. But through the magic of a pen and some notebook paper, I once again made a new friend. And we realized we had a lot in common, despite our differences.

If you've had the privilege of traveling and exploring, whether internationally or in your hometown, maybe you've experienced this, too? Maybe you've suddenly become the minority in a new situation, even though your typical version of normal means almost everyone else looks like you. Or maybe you're usually in the minority, but you've been able to go to a place where the "normal" majority is full of people who look just like you.

As I've traveled, I've realized another thing that is all too normal around the world. The judgments that people often have about their neighbors. Whether it's city dwellers shaming the suburbanites or citizens of one country looking down upon the folks across the border, this behavior is as normal as it gets. I once visited Belgium with my family. My sister had a friend from Belgium who had been an exchange student at her school, and during our visit, her friend's dad was graciously giving us a tour of their country. While we stopped to explore a local attraction, the father spotted a group of colorfully dressed tourists and said they looked weird, noting that "They must be from the Netherlands." I realized that no matter where you go, people often tend to look down upon each other. Even if they're only a little bit different and live nearby. Around the world, people are questioning each other's version of normal and judging them as weird.

Normal Is A Spectrum

How might we be more curious about trying to understand somebody else's definition of "normal," instead of judging their lives by our definition of "normal"?

Normal is a spectrum. And so are most aspects of life. But instead, we want everything to be this or that... yes or no... right or wrong.

We're uncomfortable swimming in the uncertainty. So many controversial topics have become stark shades of black versus white, where there is no room for nuance. But in reality, life is usually played out in so many shades of grey.

Here in the United States, our country has become so polarized as red versus blue. But if you tackled all of the individual issues that people care about, the way our individual opinions and values play out across the broad spectrum would be more like a United States of

Purple and Lavender. But things have become so polarized that we feel forced to choose a side. To pick one versus the other. To take a stand, and to be vocal and adamant about our opinion. To never back down or change our mind, even if the facts may change.

This type of binary thinking is an oversimplification of the human experience. Most of the people I know don't agree with *any* politician on every single issue. They choose the issues they care about most deeply and they vote based on which candidate matches their views on those most important issues. Heck, even in personal relationships — how often is it that we meet someone with whom we agree 100%? Almost never! Wouldn't life be boring if we *did* agree all the time, on everything? What would we even talk about?

How might the world be different if we approached conversations with more curiosity, *especially* when people are different from us? If we tried to understand *why* someone believes something, instead of trying to convince them to believe the same thing as us? And how might the world be different if we moved more of our conversations offline?

We're starved as a society for connection. We turn to social media platforms, thinking we'll get our fix of human connection and belonging, but we're hungrier than ever. We need face-to-face curiosity, conversation, and connection to bring us together.

Get Curious!

★ Have you ever felt weird or been called weird? Is there a particular reason why? Think about that reason — in what ways might it be pretty "normal" or common?

★ What are the reasons you typically judge other people before getting to know them? Is it because of the way they look, how they talk, or their political leanings? Next time you meet someone like this, try pressing "pause" before judging them. How might you approach their differences or your own thoughts with more curiosity?

★ Have a curious and vulnerable conversation with a friend. Ask them about their experiences — have they ever felt weird or like they didn't belong? Why? As they share their experiences, don't interrupt. Let them share their story without commentary and when they're done, thank them for opening up to you.

★ Be a local explorer! Take a walk or drive through a nearby neighborhood you've never visited, visit a place of worship for a religion other than your own, or eat a type of cuisine you've never tried before. What do you notice?

★ Are you familiar with the concepts of "unconscious bias" and "cultural conditioning?" The environments in which we are raised, including our families, school, religious or spiritual upbringing, and overall culture influence our thoughts on both a conscious and unconscious level. They shape our concepts of what is "weird" versus what is "normal." What beliefs or ideas do you hold that are truly your own and which ones have you inherited from your upbringing? Are there any beliefs or ideas that you are ready to get rid of?

★ If you feel resistant to these activities, pause. Notice what you're feeling in your body and wonder, "Why am I feeling this way?"

WHEEL OF WEIRD

compassion

The Pursuit of Happiness... Or the Pursuit of Self-Compassion?

We often pursue the idea of happiness. But happiness is fleeting. And what is happiness anyway?

For a long time, I thought I was pretty happy. And in many ways, I was. I'm a fairly optimistic person, although I definitely have my cynical, skeptical side. But despite this surface-level happiness, I would find myself beating myself up and talking to myself in ways that I would never talk to another person. It wasn't until the last few years that I started learning to be more self-compassionate.

I started going to therapy for the first time in my life a couple of years ago. I went to my first therapist for couples counseling. My 14-year relationship was beginning to crumble and my partner and I started seeing a therapist, both together and in solo sessions, to try to salvage the relationship. After a bumpy eight months of that, I got a recommendation from a close friend of mine for a different therapist. In my first tear-filled session with him, I poured my heart out, explained everything that had been going on and how I was feeling. This therapy session felt different than my previous ones. Here, I'd found someone who listened, asked questions, and noticed the physical manifestations of what I was feeling on the inside. I didn't feel judged or as if someone was trying to diagnose me. Instead, I felt seen, heard, and understood. Within the next 24 hours after leaving that therapy session, I knew what I had to do: I had to end my relationship for good.

How I would do that was another matter, of course, and it was made even more difficult by another curveball only two days later. I found out that my full-time, salaried position as Director of Marketing was becoming a part-time, contract position with no benefits, as the tech company I was working for was being split up and part of it sold off. When I heard that news, I was remarkably calm. I was a bit scared and uncertain, to be sure, but all things considered, I also felt optimism and possibility. I'd been wanting to transition into professional speaking, and I saw this as the push I needed to dive deeper into those waters. A few days after getting the news about my job, I signed up to attend a public speaking conference that would change my life forever. Finally, about three weeks after my first session with my new therapist, I packed up all of my essentials, announced to my partner that I couldn't continue the relationship anymore, and drove to my mom's house, where I'd live for the next month, before learning to live alone again for the first time since college while also working from home.

I've thought about that period of my life a lot since the COVID-19 pandemic changed life as we know it. So many people around the world were suddenly forced to learn new ways of living and working, much as I did during the summer and fall of 2018. I've found myself immensely grateful for that experience, as it prepared me to cope with many of the changes brought on by the pandemic.

During that time of transition, I spent many hours and days on my own. Even for an introvert, that was no easy task after living with a partner for nearly a decade and a half. In those quiet moments alone, I discovered the power of ritual. I learned the importance of finding my own ways to cope and finding joy in the little things. I was fortunate to live near City Park, a 1,300-acre public park in New Orleans filled with majestic centuries-old oak trees. I started going on frequent walks or runs over to the park, often listening to audiobooks or podcasts. It was here that I listened to the audiobook of *Self-Compassion: The Proven Power of Being Kind to Yourself* by Dr. Kristin Neff. I'd often find myself having to pause the audiobook, as tears streamed down my face. She discussed the differences between self-esteem versus self-compassion, and I felt it resonate with me. Growing up, I always felt like I had pretty high self-esteem. I made good grades and excelled at plenty of things I did. But at the same time, I would use harsh, negative self-talk. I would speak to myself in ways that I would NEVER speak to someone else. If something went wrong, the first place my mind went was to call myself "stupid." I may have thought highly of myself in plenty of ways, but I lacked true self-compassion.

The other thing that was interesting to me as I listened was that the research around self-compassion has shown that as people develop more self-compassion, they also start to be more compassionate towards other people as well.

Growing up, I often felt judged, particularly by my father. I felt his judgments and criticisms directed toward me, my sister, and my mom, but I also saw it directed inward, at himself. I saw him model judgmental behavior frequently, whether it was toward waitstaff or customer service professionals, or people of other ethnicities or backgrounds. We usually learn what we are taught. Luckily, my mom is one of the most generous and compassionate people I know, so judgment was not the only thing I learned growing up. But even now, further into my own journey of embracing self-compassion, I still sometimes struggle with the push and pull between my judgmental self and my compassionate self.

Another turning-point book for me was *Nonviolent Communication: A Language of Life* by Marshall B. Rosenberg, Ph.D. I found the tools for using nonviolent communication to speak to and interact with other people immensely helpful, but I realized the same tools can also apply to the way we speak to ourselves. The nonviolent communication process is focused on honestly expressing and emphatically receiving information about our observations, feelings, needs, and requests. What Rosenberg defines so clearly in his book is similar to what I felt the first time I met with my new therapist, who observed both my words and my physical responses. He then asked me questions to help me bring awareness to my feelings and needs. Through a lot of therapy and self-reflection (journaling is great for this!), as well as resources like Neff's and Rosenberg's books, I have become much more mindful of paying attention to my feelings and needs. Rather than continuing unhealthy cycles of negative self-talk, I am often able to catch myself when I find myself being judgmental, whether toward myself or others, and re-examine the unmet needs that are causing me to think or act this way.

I'm still not perfect, by any means, but practice makes progress. And while happiness may be fleeting, progress is still a move in the right direction.

Compassion: A Two-Way Street

Compassion is a two-way street. As we start to become more self-compassionate, we start to be less judgmental towards ourselves. We soften the words we use toward ourselves, which are often much harsher than the words we use toward others. As we dive deeper into self-compassion, it also becomes easier for us to be more compassionate toward other people.

I had an epiphany while listening to an episode of the podcast *The Hilarious World of Depression*. Host John Moe interviews comedians and celebrities who struggle with different mental health issues. On this particular episode was an interview with Andrew Zimmern who hosts the *Bizarre Foods* show on the Travel Channel. He's also a former drug addict and alcoholic. He said something that stopped me in my tracks:

"Trauma that is not transformed... gets transferred."

Trauma that is not transformed into something else, gets transferred to other people. The moment I heard this statement, I realized, yeah, it's so true! I realized so much of the pain and heartbreak I'd felt was transferred to me because people in my life hadn't yet been able to transform their childhood trauma. I also recognized that — like so many of us — I had traumas and pain that were transferred to me, which were causing me to act out negatively toward other people. We were continuing this cycle of trauma and pain. We were all just passing it around in this infinity symbol of suffering. When we haven't been able to transform our past trauma and begin to move past it, it gets transferred to the people around us.

When people act out toward us, it can be incredibly hard to consider at the moment that they might be coming from a place of pain. A few years ago, I experienced this firsthand. I hosted a podcast called *Badass Creatives*, which offered marketing and business advice for creative entrepreneurs. One day, I got an angry email about a certain episode, which focused on tips for selling at a craft fair. I'd sold at craft shows for more than a decade, and I'd even written a book about it. I'd tried to make this podcast episode as useful as possible, so this unexpected email caught me off guard. The woman who emailed me was very upset, and her email was pretty rude. It hurt to read her words.

My initial gut reaction was to respond and be equally rude back to her, but pretty recently before this happened, there'd been an incident that made headlines with the comedian Sarah Silverman. She had received some hateful messages, posted publicly via Twitter. Instead of immediately lashing back out at the guy, however, she took the time to dig through his Twitter feed. She saw this guy was going through some tough medical issues. Sarah Silverman realized he was acting out because he was in a place of both physical and emotional pain and he was taking it out on her. Rather than responding to his negativity with more negativity, she turned it around and reached out compassionately. She tried to make him feel heard and started a dialogue between the two of them. Via their public conversation, he shared that he'd been abused as a child. Sarah responded with genuine caring and concern, urging him to find a local support group and asking her millions of followers to help connect him with specialists for his medical issues.

So, before I responded to my own situation, I channeled my inner Sarah Silverman. I took a moment to calm myself down, then I sat down to respond to this woman's email. I tried to come from a place of compassion and understanding. I told her, "I'm sorry you're disappointed in this episode. I know it's been helpful for a lot of people. I'm sorry it wasn't helpful for you."

It also occurred to me... maybe she didn't learn best from listening. There are different learning styles. Sometimes it's hard for me to learn things only by listening — I'm a very visual person, so I thought maybe she could be similar and it might be easier for her to learn via a written format. I sent her some of my blog posts about the same topic. I also explained that I felt hurt by the way she spoke to me. I told her, "I know for you to have spoken to me in that way means you must have some sort of pain in your life right now. I am deeply sorry for whatever you're going through. I hope you find healing soon."

I sent the email... and then... within a few hours, she responded. She apologized for speaking to me that way. (Which is not the response I expected to get!) She said, "Yeah, you're right. I'm sorry I lashed out at you." She explained that her boyfriend just dumped her. In the introduction of that particular episode, I'd talked about my boyfriend at the time and how he was getting ready for his first craft show. Hearing me talk about him had upset her since she was going through a breakup.

This idea of responding to hurt and pain with compassion is something I've thought a lot about. I try to practice it as much as possible, but I'm certainly not perfect. I still have those moments where my gut reaction is, "Oh my god, you're so stupid and annoying and I want to punch you in the face right now." But I try to catch myself, checking in with myself compassionately and then trying to find compassion for the other person.

One tool I love is a meditative practice centered around compassion toward others. When I started going to therapy, my therapist recommended a book called *When Things Fall Apart* by Pema Chödrön, a Buddhist nun. In this book, she explains a practice called Tonglen, which is a meditative practice for sending and receiving compassion. For me, I know that the thing I need most is self-compassion, but when we've always been really hard on ourselves, practicing self-compassion — especially at the beginning — can feel like an impossible task. Tonglen resonated with me because it flips compassion on its head. It forces you to think about the pain of others first. During a Tonglen meditation, we breathe in the pain of others. It's the same kind of pain we're going through ourselves, but rather than focusing on our pain, we focus first on bringing healing to others. As we breathe out, we send out waves of relief and healing to other people who are experiencing the same types of painful feelings as us. For example, if you've felt shame and judgment, you don't wallow in your feelings. You think about all of the other people in the world who are going through the same thing as you. As you breathe in, you imagine breathing in all of their pain. But as you breathe out, you imagine sending out waves of light and healing and joy to the whole wide world. It's kind of like becoming a spiritual superhero!

How might we soften the way that we treat ourselves, the way we speak to ourselves? How

might we offer ourselves a bit more compassion,
so that we can pay it forward to others?

Imagine Compassion

As I've learned to practice more compassion toward myself, I've found my heart softening towards others too. Extending compassion toward other people who have caused harm does *not* excuse their misdeeds. But when we tap into the power of compassion, we connect with our common humanity. We may realize that the *why* of what caused someone to harm another person is not all that different from the *why* of what causes us pain, too.

I invite you to imagine a time when someone made you feel judged or like you didn't belong. Were you ever bullied in school? Has anyone ever made you feel inadequate or not good enough? Maybe the person who made you feel this way was a parent, friend, teacher, boss, or romantic partner?

As you think back, I invite you to reflect on how it made you feel. If you are the journaling type, you might want to take some time to sit quietly and write about your memories of this situation. Or maybe you'd rather take a walk as you think about this time in your life.

Consider the person or people who made you feel this way. Did their actions or words change your relationship with them? As you reflect on this, ask yourself this as well, "What else do I know about the person who hurt my feelings? Is there any reason why they might have acted out so negatively?"

Again, it's important to note that whatever pain or harm someone else may have experienced does *not* give them an excuse to continue to inflict pain on you or anyone else. But as we learn to exercise our compassion muscles, I invite you to consider any pain that person may have been feeling themselves. Try to think about their pain through a compassionate lens, much like you might offer yourself self-compassion.

Next, I invite you to think about a time when *you've* been judgmental toward someone. (We've all done this at some point. Being judgmental occasionally is a very human experience. I'm sure even the Dalai Lama has moments of passing judgment toward other people.) Think about a time when you've been judgmental toward someone else. Perhaps a co-worker or a family member? Or maybe it's a certain type of person you encounter online, whether on social media or in the comments section of a news website. You know, the type of person who always seems to get under your skin?

I invite you to consider if there are any similarities between the reasons why you find yourself judging other people and why you have felt judged by other people in the past. If you frequently judge other people as stupid idiots, have you felt insecure about your own "stupid mistakes" or not feeling smart enough? (This one is definitely me, by the way! For years, anytime anything would go wrong in my life, I would call myself stupid and beat myself up for not knowing better, even if there's no way I possibly could have known! Being "stupid" or not smart enough was the #1 way I judged myself, but it was also the primary way I found myself judging other people, too.)

These days, when I find myself feeling low and judging myself or other people, I try to remember the wise words of Don Miguel Ruiz from his book *The Four Agreements*. As he describes the fourth agreement, "Always Do Your Best," he reminds us that your best will change over time, depending on how you are feeling physically and emotionally. But we can always try to do our best and give it our all, with the physical, mental, and emotional resources we have available to us in each moment. We can also pause to remember that pretty much everyone else is doing the same. I believe that most people are good at heart, but we are children of cultures, schooling, and systems that we spend the rest of our lives unlearning and unpacking. We're all at different points in that journey. You wouldn't expect the same things from a kindergartener that you would from a college student. We're all doing the best we can, with what we have, where we're at during each moment in life. We're all human, we all make mistakes, but we all just keep trying. Be gentle and kind to yourself today, and be kind to others, too.

Cultivate Compassion!

★ Think about a time when you've said or done something that may have been hurtful to someone else. What were you feeling at the time? How do you feel about that situation now? Do you have any regrets? What did you learn from that experience?

★ Consider a situation in which someone else said or did something hurtful to you. Have you forgiven them yet? If not, why? If you still feel anger or resentment towards them, how is that anger or resentment beneficial to you or harmful to you? Forgiveness and compassion do not make excuses for the harm created by another, but they can offer healing comfort to ourselves.

★ Are you hard on yourself? Do you ever speak unkindly or belittle yourself? If you struggle with being self-compassionate, imagine yourself as a very young child, perhaps five years old. How would you talk to and encourage the child version of yourself?

★ Have you ever spoken with a therapist or shared your experiences with a support group? When we can open up and be emotionally vulnerable with other human beings in a safe space, we connect with our common humanity and begin to heal. How are you currently taking care of your mental health?

WHEEL OF WEIRD

authenticity

Your Authentic Spark

How might we fully accept and embrace our authentic selves, as well as accept the authentic truth about others? How might we embrace our weird, and, in turn, embrace the weird of others?

Many of us have pushed down an authentic part of ourselves to fit the mold we thought others wanted us to fit into. But if somebody is inauthentic, we often judge them as fake. Whether unconsciously or consciously, we don't like fake people. It's a vicious cycle: We start to become inauthentic because we want to be liked. Instead of truly being ourselves, we try to become the people we think other people want us to be. But in doing so, we create the opposite reaction: We become more unlikeable. When someone seems to be inauthentic, we distance ourselves from them. We may even judge them as "weird."

Authenticity requires a curious understanding of who we are. What is your authentic spark? Your "weird"? What is your unique combination of strengths and weaknesses, experiences and talents that you bring to the world that no one else can? And how are you going to share that with the people around you?

How each of us explores, understands, and embraces our authentic selves will be different for everyone. There's no one right way because we're all beautifully weird in our own ways, so we gotta find what works for us.

This sounds so cheesy, but one thing that's helped me understand the strengths I can share with those around me is personality tests. I'm not talking about those *Cosmopolitan* magazine quizzes like, "This Wedding Dress Test Will Tell You Who To Marry" or those Facebook memes that tell you which Harry Potter house you belong to. Instead, I mean the kind of personality tests that hone in on your strengths and weaknesses.

The first one I ever took was, coincidentally, called *StrengthsFinder*. The company I was working for made all of us take the quiz and read the accompanying book. There are 34 different strengths, and the quiz identifies your top five. I learned that my top strength is **Futuristic**, which has been both a strength *and* weakness for me. People with the Futuristic strength are "inspired by the future and what could be." It means I'm ambitious and driven by long-term goals, but it can also mean I worry about the future a lot. I tend to worry about important big-picture things like climate change, but I also stress about mundane things that aren't worth worrying about at all. It was mind-blowing for me when I discovered this because I realized, "Oh my gosh, this was the source of all of my childhood anxiety about the first day of school and how I thought they weren't gonna give me my schedule or tell me where to go, and that I was going to have to figure it out magically somehow..." While being future-focused has been a source of anxiety for me, it's also the thing that helps me envision a better, brighter world and see the possibility in things.

Another one of my top strengths is **Learner**, which explains my natural curiosity and desire to gobble up information. People with the Learner strength enjoy the process of learning itself, and they get excited about self-improvement and figuring things out. I also found out that I'm a **Maximizer**, which means that I tend to focus on my existing strengths rather than trying to improve my weakest skills. I'm a hard worker, but if something doesn't come easily to me, I tend to cut my losses and give up. I'd rather spend my time diving deeper into my natural talents and abilities. Learning about my Maximizer strength led to another revelation: All of those times I quit something, like my sixth-grade soccer team or when I stopped playing saxophone in the high school band... it wasn't because I was lazy. It was because those weren't things that fully brought me alive. They weren't things I was naturally great at or enjoyed doing. Because when there are things that spark joy and bring me fully alive? I go *all the way in*.

When it comes to our authentic needs within personal relationships, there's a book and quiz called *The Five Love Languages*. Maybe you've heard of it? The love languages are Words of Affirmation, Quality Time, Receiving Gifts, Acts of Service, and Physical Touch, and when you take the quiz, you'll learn where on the spectrum you fall for each of these. Most people enjoy each of these to some extent. Understanding your primary love languages as well as the primary love languages of the people closest to you can help you communicate your needs better. Whether it's expressing love and affection with a romantic partner or with friends and family, becoming aware of your love languages can truly help build connections between people. (I should have taken this quiz when I was still with my ex.)

Another thing that helped me better understand my own authentic needs and desires was cultivating a daily gratitude practice. In 2018, I embarked on a daily project. I shared my #yearofgratitude project publicly via Instagram and Facebook. The end of 2017 was a rough time, and at the beginning of the new year, I was looking for something to get me back on track and help me feel better.

I'd also gotten myself into this inauthentic rut when it came to my social media accounts. By this time, I had worked in marketing for so long that I'd created all of these "shoulds" for myself about what I was supposed to be doing on social media. A few years before that, however, I used to see Instagram as a medium of artistic expression. I would find joy in taking these little square photos on my phone, and I'd share them along with captions I would think of as creative writing projects. But I'd gotten myself into this rut where I wasn't doing that anymore. The year before I did this daily project, I barely posted. At the start of this project, I looked back through Instagram and in 2017 I'd only shared something like 40 posts the whole year, and half of those weren't even photos taken that year! I'd just been re-posting stuff that had gotten a bunch of likes previously. I'd started caring way too much about what other people thought. I needed something to help me break the shackles of all these self-imposed "shoulds" and reconnect with my authentic self.

I'd also read a lot about the transformative power of gratitude. There are a ton of studies showing how practicing acts of gratitude can improve our happiness as well as our relationships with others. Reminding yourself to be grateful for what you have, even if it's as simple as, "I woke up today! I have food to eat! I'm still alive!" — these conscious acts of gratitude can be immensely valuable in so many ways.

There were a lot of days during 2018 when I really needed this daily gratitude practice. I'm truly grateful for embarking on my #yearofgratitude project at the beginning of that year, because by the summer I left my long-term relationship, lost my full-time job, and my dog died — all within one month. Cultivating gratitude daily and sharing those gratitude posts publicly helped me get through a really painful year, and I know it helped others, too. Not only was I getting likes and comments on Facebook and Instagram, but so many people reached out to me or mentioned it in person, both during that year and since then. Some of these were people who never commented or liked any of the posts on social media, but they still saw the posts. They told me in person how much my project meant to them and how inspired by it they were. Some of them even started their own daily gratitude projects, which was super cool!

Whether you choose to do it publicly like I did or whether you write in a journal or reflect privately on what you're grateful for, how can you use gratitude when you're feeling critical toward yourself or feeling judged or bullied by the people in your life?

Speaking of the people in your life, who are the people you feel like you can be your most authentic self around? Who makes you feel unconditionally accepted? Who *never* makes you feel judged?

And on the flip side... who *does* make you feel judged? How might you design your life to include more time with the people who make you feel authentically you? And how might you limit your interaction with those who make you feel judged?

Who Were You, Before the World Changed You?

Who are you, at your core? And who were you, before the world changed you? When you were born, perfect and complete. What were you like back then? Before the expectations of parents, grandparents, teachers, and friends layered on top of your core being, smothering and trying to stamp out that first authentic spark within?

In our childhood, we become shaped by the expectations of others. We often start to become inauthentic versions of ourselves to fit in, be liked, belong, survive. Middle school and our teenage years are especially rough when it comes to this. Puberty throws all sorts of hormones at us, making us act in unexpected ways. Then we go through the high school years testing out and trying on the interests and habits of others as we try to figure out where we fit into the world.

For many of us, there is a breaking point somewhere in adulthood. An existential crisis. A series of life-altering events that cause us to stop and re-examine who we've become along the way. Are we the people we want to be, or some hazy, muddled version of ourselves shaped by the expectations of others?

For me, that moment started right before my 35th birthday. Back when I was 20, I started dating somebody that I would end up spending the next decade and a half of my life with. If you had told me that only a few years prior, in high school, I would never have believed it.

In many ways, it was a good relationship. That's why I stayed in it for so long. But in other ways, I lost part of myself. My partner was 10 years older than me, and when we started dating a few weeks before I turned 20, my list of past romantic and sexual relationships was few, whereas his was fairly numerous. I learned so many things throughout that relationship from him and with him. But over the years I also found myself adjusting my views and shifting my perspective on certain things. I don't blame him entirely for that. Part of growing up and becoming an adult is examining, "What is my way of understanding the world? What do I believe, separately from what my parents, teachers, and other people in my life have told me to believe?"

In retrospect, one aspect of myself that I feel that I pushed down, that I quieted and dampened to try to belong to that relationship, is my spirituality. Growing up, my family was never super religious. We went to church occasionally, but it was never a big part of my life as a kid. When I started dating my ex, I quickly discovered that he was a very staunch and vocal atheist. Since I was never super religious growing up, and I also knew that my grandfather was agnostic, I didn't have a problem with my ex's atheism. As long as someone else's beliefs don't cause them to inflict harm upon other people or living creatures, I think they should be allowed to determine what belief system is authentic for them.

My ex never asked me to change my beliefs for him. But sometimes it felt like he was so vocal and adamant about his already-formed opinions that I felt like I couldn't continue to explore that part of myself or share that part of myself with him. Eventually, I gave up. I stopped trying, and I buried that part of myself deep down and hid it away. I didn't want to deal with confrontation. I was still in the process of exploring and re-examining my belief systems, but he was already so strongly entrenched in his own that it felt uncomfortable to have those conversations turn into a debate in my own house.

Since leaving him, however, I have once again started exploring what spirituality means to me. In the process of healing from that breakup and trying to find my way in the world as a newly single person, I found myself attending occasional church services at a local Unitarian Universalist church. I found myself reading books about Buddhism and starting to practice yoga and meditation more frequently. I was drawn to walks in nature, enchanted with the idea of forest bathing. My walks through City Park in New Orleans under ancient oak trees became part of my healing process. I would travel to Barataria Preserve, just a 30-minute drive from downtown New Orleans, where I could walk through the wetlands. As I walked along the trails, past cypress trees and palmetto plants, I would see birds, lizards, snakes, and the occasional alligator. That communion with nature was a huge part of what helped me heal and reconnect with my authentic self.

For me, being in nature has become a huge part of my spirituality and connection with the divine. As I started getting back into running on a semi-regular basis, one day I found myself compelled to touch one of the ancient oak trees in City Park. Each time I would run past it, I felt compelled, again and again, to reach out, to touch it. I started saying hello and blowing kisses to the tree as I ran past. I found out later that particular tree is more than 700 years old. It's one of the oldest trees in City Park. I started to think about all of the things that the tree has seen. How that tree was alive and rooted here in this place that I call home before European colonial settlers ever set foot on this continent. How that tree was born centuries before Black people were taken forcibly from their homelands and brought across an ocean, enslaved. My relationship with this tree awakened a new type of spiritual experience for me.

As I found myself exploring and reacquainting myself with my spiritual side, I also began to reflect back on what other parts of myself I'd quieted and pushed down over the years. When I was in that relationship, there were many things that I hesitated to do or hesitated to have conversations about for fear of judgment. I was afraid to use my voice fully about certain topics, especially when they were topics that I was still trying to understand, but that I knew my partner had already formed opinions about. He often seemed unwilling to change. But I wanted to be able to approach things with curiosity. I wanted to be able to explore them and try to understand them. And a true sense of curiosity takes a willingness to sometimes admit that you've been wrong. It takes a willingness to change your perspective and opinion when new information or experiences are presented before you. But if you have shut down the curious, playful side of yourself, out of fear or self-preservation... or if you are surrounded by others who have, it can be hard to stay curious. If you are filled with judgmental thoughts, whether toward yourself or other people, it may feel like there is no room left for curiosity.

Unresolved trauma can be transferred, and so can judgment. We feel judged by others, so in turn, we judge ourselves. Because we continue to judge ourselves, we then judge others more harshly. It's a vicious cycle.

I didn't want to be judged, especially by the person I'd chosen to spend my life with. So I quieted certain parts of myself and hid them away. In doing so, I became an inauthentic version of myself. I was operating at 70% capacity. I couldn't bring my full self to that relationship.

In the last few years of my relationship, I started to do things on my own more often. As I started to grow my speaking business, I applied for more conferences to speak at and attend. When I was away from my partner for a few days at a conference, I found myself feeling like I could share and express parts of myself that I often kept locked away. At one conference, I stayed a few extra days so that I could go hiking in Joshua Tree National Park and visit Salvation Mountain (a larger-than-life testament to one man's quest for spirituality). At these events, I enjoyed having conversations with many different people, from a wide range of places, backgrounds, and perspectives. Every time I was away on my own having those kinds of conversations, I felt like I was tapping into my innate sense of curiosity and wonderment. I felt freer of judgment in those moments. I began to feel closer to freedom from judgment, from both myself and other people. The more I did that, the more I wanted that feeling full time.

It took a while to unravel and explore all of my feelings. Unconsciously, the end of that relationship was a few years in the making. Facing the truth that I had to end it was one of the hardest things I have ever done. But tapping into *my* authentic truth and being able to learn to live with less judgment toward myself was ultimately one of the most powerful and most fulfilling things that I have ever done.

Guilty Pleasures

If there's one thing I've never really understood, it's the idea of "guilty pleasures." Like... if it's pleasurable... *Why* do you have to feel guilty about enjoying it?!?

(Obviously, there are a few exceptions to this. For instance, if your guilty pleasure is murdering puppies or something else that harms another living creature, then yes, you should *definitely* feel very guilty about that.)

But what if your guilty pleasure is the fact that you love disco music or Broadway musicals or playing Dungeons & Dragons or any other thing that society has deemed "uncool" or out of style? (By the way, I love disco music, Broadway musicals, and D&D!) If the guilt of your guilty pleasures comes from the fact that someone, somewhere decided that the thing that brings you joy doesn't spark the same joy in them... can we collectively take a vow to stop feeling guilty about guilty pleasures? I invite you to repeat this vow out loud: "I solemnly swear to not feel guilty for things that bring me joy. And I solemnly swear to respect the things that bring joy to others, as long as they do not bring harm."

Maybe you've heard the phrases, "Don't yuck my yum" or "One person's trash is another person's treasure." We don't all have to like the same things, but we don't have to give each other grief for liking things that are different than what we like either. Rather than making assumptions about what we will or won't like before we try it, can we evoke a spirit of curiosity when it comes to new or different things? We might try something and still not enjoy it, but maybe we'll be pleasantly surprised. And even if it's not *our* thing, we can still respect that it brings someone else pleasure.

Reality Testing

We also have to be willing to listen when other people share their authentic truth with us. For instance, if someone shares their pronouns or gender identity with you, and perhaps it's different from what you expected or assumed... Or maybe they have an invisible illness, like chronic pain... How might you use curiosity and compassion to help you respect their authentic truth?

As humans, we often have trouble understanding how someone else's experience of reality may be different than ours. How whatever they've experienced in life or whatever they're going through currently might change how they interpret our words or actions. This can lead to all sorts of miscommunication.

In psychology, there's a concept that Sigmund Freud originally came up with called **reality testing**. Reality testing is basically how we learn to separate our inner world, the way *we* see the world, from what is objectively true in the outside world.

Our version and experience of the way things happen may not be the same as someone else's. We usually don't experience the world exactly the same way as other people do. Each one of us is shaped by all of our past experiences, and what we've felt so far in life up to this current moment impacts how we experience the present. When we have experienced certain difficulties in life — whether that's growing up with an abusive or alcoholic parent or experiencing microaggressions throughout life in the form of racism or misogyny... — those experiences will influence the way we react to the world around us.

Coming back to those mindsets of curiosity and compassion, how might we be more mindful about listening and trying to respect the authentic experiences of others?

Authentic Values

Authenticity also means being in alignment with your true values. Every day, we have opportunities to make choices and live in alignment with our values. But to do so, we have to first understand what matters most to us.

Our authentic values, our internal code of ethics, might be different from what our family of origin raised us with. It might be different than what society tells us. It might even be different than what is legal. Because, after all, remember that slavery was once legal. Concentration camps were once legal.

Returning to the mindsets of curiosity and compassion... Forgetting what you've been told you should value or care about... What are your core values? What does living an authentic life look like for you? And what would it mean to live by your authentic values each and every day?

Rather than simply calling yourself an ally or activist, how will you take a stand? How will you take action to live in alignment with your authentic truth and your core values?

Embrace Authenticity!

★ Who were you as a child? What did you love to do and explore when you were young? Were there any experiences that made you stop doing the things you loved as a child? As we grow older, it is natural for our interests and beliefs to evolve. Often this growth is healthy, but sometimes outside forces or other people force us to change in ways that don't truly align with who we are or what we want. Are there any aspects of who you were as a child that you'd like to reconnect with?

★ What beliefs, ideas, and "cultural conditioning" are you holding on to that are inherited from your upbringing? Are there any people in your life who have known you since childhood that you could talk with about this? Perhaps a parent, sibling, childhood friend, aunt, or uncle? Sometimes by talking with the people who have known us the longest we can uncover puzzle pieces that help us make sense of our past and how we became the person we are today.

★ Start a daily gratitude practice or gratitude journal. If you prefer writing, grab a notebook and before you go to bed each night, write down a few things you were grateful for that day. You could also incorporate this practice with another daily activity. Reflect on what you're grateful for each day while you brush your teeth or eat your breakfast. Try to stick with this habit for at least one week at first, then one month. Once you've been practicing gratitude regularly for a while, notice how you feel. Do you feel calmer or more content?

★ Are there parts of yourself that you keep hidden, perhaps even from those closest to you? Why? What would it take to make you feel safe and comfortable sharing these parts of yourself with someone else?

★ What are your core values and beliefs? When did you first know them to be true and important to you? Who or what played a role in developing these values and

beliefs? How have your values and beliefs changed over time?

WHEEL OF WEIRD

action

Action vs Allyship

When I first created the Wheel of Weird, this final section had a different name. Originally, it was called **Allyship**.

To be an ally to someone else... That's an important piece of this whole diversity and inclusion thing, right? Yes, it is. But the more I thought about it and the more I considered this concept not just in my head but also with my heart, I realized that allyship was the wrong word to use. If you look at some of the definitions of **ally**... it means "to cooperate with," "to help," and "to side with or support." Those are all great starting places, of course. But they're just that: a start.

We think a lot about allyship in terms of showing up as an ally for somebody else — someone of a different race or sexual orientation or gender identity. And yes, we should strive to be allies for people who are different from us. But before we can be allies to others, we have to start by being allies to ourselves — friends to ourselves first — before we can show up as true allies for others. If we haven't done our internal work first or if we haven't had our own basic human needs met, it's hard for us to be fully present as an ally and take action toward creating a kinder, more inclusive world.

If we haven't done the work of unpacking our own unconscious bias and cultural conditioning, our allyship and actions may become performative. Fake. Inauthentic. If we haven't begun to move past our pain or heal our trauma, we might end up passing our pain on to others. But when we've done the internal work, offering ourselves compassion and embracing our authentic strengths throughout the process, we can become more effective co-conspirators in the movements toward equity and justice for everyone.

With so much talk about diversity, equity, and inclusion these days, sometimes people hear the word "ally" and think of it as a label that they can give themselves. But that's not how it works. Becoming an ally is the direct result of taking **action**. We must take action to heal ourselves

and to create a more equitable and inclusive
world.

Being An Ally To Yourself

If we want to create a kinder, more inclusive world, we can't only look outward and expect other people to change. Changing the world starts with changing ourselves.

Taking action to be kinder to yourself can create a ripple effect. As you learn to be kinder and gentler with yourself, you will likely be able to extend that compassion to the people around you.

I can be incredibly hard on myself sometimes. I've said things to myself that I would never say to a friend. If something goes wrong, the first place my mind often goes is to call myself stupid. (Even though I know I'm not stupid!) But the negative part of my brain goes there immediately. And I'm pretty sure I'm not the only one. A lot of really smart, extremely competent people feel this way. They feel like frauds, phonies, imposters, and inadequate. Maybe you've felt this way at some point?

I'm still a work in progress. We all are. Going to therapy has been tremendously helpful for me, both in healing and in beginning to unpack some of my cultural conditioning. These days, finding a therapist is more accessible than ever, with many different online therapy options to choose from in addition to traditional counseling services.

For many people, finding a support group of individuals dealing with similar issues is the key that unlocks the door to healing. Programs like Alcoholics Anonymous and Al-Anon (which offer support to the families and friends of people who have alcoholism and other addictions) have offered life-saving support and helped countless people around the world.

Journaling, whether you do it in the traditional written format or by recording voice memos on your phone, can also be a great way to explore and unravel the layers of inherited beliefs that we may or may not still believe in ourselves. **Leesa Renée Hall** is an anti-bias facilitator and mental wellness advocate who helps people unpack unconscious biases through the use of reflective writing prompts. In 2019, I attended a workshop she hosted in New York City, and I am also a member of her Patreon community. Her *Inner Field Trip* ® program and writing prompts are particularly useful for people who identify as empaths, introverts, or highly sensitive.

As you progress in your healing journey, you may find yourself wanting to do more to help others and heal the world. The past few years have brought more awareness to the injustices of the world. In the wake of the murder of George Floyd at the hands of police in May 2020, the internet was awash in anti-racist reading lists. These book lists offered a starting point, but a few months later, how many of these books that were purchased in haste, out of a sense of guilt by many white people, lingered on bookshelves and bedside tables, unread?

When injustice makes the news, there is often a sense of urgency. Of all-or-nothing, fix-it-now, binary thinking. As if we could fix the problems created over hundreds of years in the blink of an eye. The work of creating a more equitable world, of putting an end to archaic systems of oppression, is not fast. It is not quick or easy. It is the work of a lifetime, of all of our lifetimes. To be an ally to ourselves as we embark on this work means not trying to make the journey alone. Yes, we can read books alone, listen to a podcast, or watch a lecture, but we also need to find support and community. And when it comes to the work of anti-oppression and healing the world of injustice, those of us with identities of power and/or privilege must look to the people with historically marginalized identities to lead. We must be willing to listen and learn. We must stay curious and be humble. We must be willing to step down from positions of power when necessary and make room for other voices to be heard. And we must show ourselves grace and compassion because we will almost certainly make mistakes as we stumble toward a more inclusive and equitable world.

Everyday Actions

Taking impactful action might sound overwhelming at first. But there are plenty of everyday actions you can take at work, at home, and in your daily life.

Some of my favorite resources for learning about this come in the form of free email newsletters. You can join 250,000+ subscribers when you sign up for **Anti-Racism Daily** (ARD), a free daily newsletter aimed at dismantling white supremacy. You can find archives at the ARD website along with action steps for each topic. Another favorite of mine comes from Karen Catlin, the founder and author of *Better Allies*. Each Friday she sends a **5 Ally Actions** email filled with super actionable, real-life examples that you can start using right away to create a more inclusive workplace and world. Her Instagram is also a great place to pick up tips.

There are so many people these days who use Instagram and other social media platforms to share helpful tips on how to be more inclusive. Another Instagram favorite of mine is **Blair Imani**, an award-winning educator, author, and influencer. Through her "Smarter in Seconds" series, she educates her followers on different issues around diversity and inclusion and shares specific ways to take action. She also dives deeper into these topics on YouTube and in her books.

Learning how to be a better ally and how to take action is a lifelong process. We are all at different stages of this journey. As I continue along my path, I try to stay curious and open. It's important to remember that *we don't know what we don't know*, but we can always keep learning.

When I started along this path, one of the first things I realized I needed to pay more attention to was, "Who is not here, and why?"

This can be interpreted in many ways, depending on your lifestyle and background. You might ask yourself, "Who is not in my circle of friends, or network of professional contacts? Why?" You could also examine the media you consume. When it comes to the types of movies or TV shows you watch, or who you follow on Instagram or your social media channel of choice... who is not there... and why? You can ask yourself while looking around your workplace or neighborhood. You might also think back to your upbringing and childhood education. Whose stories were missing from the books you read in school? What types of people did you rarely interact with in person during your formative years?

If you look around and find that your community, workplace, or even social media feed is filled primarily with people who are very similar to you, how might you diversify your own experience of the world? How might you get to know people in your local community who come from different backgrounds? Could you add a few movies created by underrepresented filmmakers to your Netflix queue?

The more we can surround ourselves with diverse perspectives, the more we start to learn about other people's versions of "normal" and their lived experiences. As we have more curious conversations with people from different backgrounds, we become more aware of the many everyday actions we could take to be more inclusive of other people.

Unexpected Actions

There are so many everyday ways to be an ally when you open yourself to the possibilities. But sometimes they come in the most unexpected places. For instance, a few years ago I discovered a way that I could use my *weird* to be an ally on the dance floor.

Think back... maybe you once attended a middle school or high school dance where no one was dancing? Even though maybe some people wanted to, they were too worried about what other people would think? This happened to me a few years ago at a conference. There was a designated dance floor area where everyone gathered in the evenings, but on the first night of the conference, no one was dancing.

One woman walked up to me and said, "Gosh, I *really* want to dance. But I don't want to be the first person on the dance floor." The whole night went by, and no one danced. The music played and the conference schedule made it clear that this time and place was designated for dancing, but still, no one danced.

The following night, they had this special event where you could sign up to host a workshop, impromptu. I decided to host an "improvisational dancing" session in the same area where the dancing was *supposed* to happen the previous night. Lo and behold, this time people showed up. Suddenly, they felt like they had permission to dance.

More and more people joined, and they danced with me. I soon realized that I needed to put all of my energy into dancing because my energy was fueling this dance party. I had become the hype girl for this dance party, and by being willing to act silly and let loose, everyone else was free to do so too. No one was alone on the dance floor that night.

I had so much fun dancing that night, and I got really into it. But after a while, I started getting exhausted. I don't do that much cardio regularly, and all the dancing was taking its toll. I was afraid to stop dancing or leave the dance floor to sit down though because if I did, everyone else might stop dancing too. Then I had an idea! I got down on the carpeted dance floor and rolled around on my back, with my legs and arms flailing around in the air. I've since dubbed this dance move the "Stranded Turtle." I was able to rest a bit but I was still on the dance floor and still dancing, in a weird way. But the truly weird thing was that after I started doing this, I looked around and other people started doing the same thing! We were all rolling around on the floor, flailing like stranded tortoises with our legs and arms pointed sky high. Somehow my decision that it was okay to look and act ridiculous made other people feel like they could act silly and have fun, too.

My moment of unexpected action on the dance floor may be a silly one, but the truth is, it did create belonging and connection that night. Whether it's an example like mine or speaking up when you witness injustice or behavior that could be hurtful to someone else... How can we step up and be the first person to put ourselves out there? How can we take a risk so that others feel safe making the leap, too? Whether it's being silly or being brave, taking action can give other people the courage to act as well.

Take Action!

★ Based on your core values and beliefs, what is one thing you wish you could change in your local community? Are there any people or organizations currently working to make an impact and create change in this area? In what ways could you use your strengths and skills to contribute to this cause?

★ What is one problem in the world that you want to understand better? Maybe you've heard terms like "disability justice," "decolonization," or "environmental racism" but you don't know what they mean. Do you have any friends or family who might be interested in the same topic? Invite them to join you in learning more together.

★ How diverse is the media you consume? What would it look like to expand the types of movies or TV shows you watch or the authors you read? Could you challenge yourself to read one article a week or watch one documentary a month written or created by an underrepresented artist?

★ Get involved in a mutual aid network. Unlike traditional charity, mutual aid is about cooperation. Think: people helping people for the sake of the common good. Volunteer your time or donate money. You might even ask a friend to join your efforts. Search "mutual aid" online to find local networks near you and learn more.

EMBRACE YOUR WEIRD

Creating A Kinder, More Inclusive World

We are the weird ones. And we are the normal ones, too. We, the humans, are united in our weirdness *and* our normality. By using the Wheel of Weird and cultivating Curiosity, Compassion, Authenticity, and Action, we can better embrace our own weird as we also delight in the weird of others. We can create a kinder, more inclusive world, together.

Embracing your weird means getting curious about those parts of ourselves we've been made to feel ashamed about. What we've pushed down and hidden away because of the judgment we've felt or feared from the outer world. Embracing your weird means showing yourself compassion and accepting your authentic truth. It also means taking mindful action and being kinder to yourself.

Embracing *their* weird extends these same principles toward other people. It often starts with curiosity, because as we become more curious and have open-hearted conversations with others who are different from us, we can learn and accept the authentic truth about them as well. We can begin to extend compassion towards other people. Once we've established a basis of curiosity, compassion, and authenticity, we can take action to create a more inclusive and equitable world.

So much of the anger, distrust, and bullying in the world come from people who are actively hurting. The judgments that we have toward other people are so often a reflection of the judgments we have toward ourselves. People who have cultivated true self-awareness and self-compassion don't usually seek to create pain in the lives of others. But when we feel hurt and judged by others, we often continue the cycle, spewing pain and judgment toward other people in return.

We all want to belong. We all want to feel loved. This quest for belonging, the need to fit in with a group, is so innately human.

This is something else I've wondered about. I try to imagine myself tens of thousands of years ago, in prehistoric times. Back then, if your tribe thought that you were too weak, not good enough, or even maybe too weird, they might cast you out. A life alone as an outcast in those ancient times could literally mean your death. When we think about inclusion and belonging, whether in our daily lives or the workplace, we can't forget there is this deeply human part of us that *needs* to belong.

To find belonging for ourselves, we help create belonging for others. To be more inclusive of others, we begin by embracing our differences and healing our own hurt. We must start from a place of self-compassion and also extend compassion toward others. We must seek to understand the pain others have felt, and seek the common humanity in our pain. It's not a matter of judging whose pain is greater or more valid because there is no Pain Olympics. None of us is exempt from pain or hurt. We all experience pain, both physical and emotional, of some type throughout our lives. And while our pain can come from so many different sources and some of us may, unfortunately, experience more pain than others, the *way* we human beings feel pain is so similar.

Our "weird" is so often the thing we've been made to feel ashamed about. It's what we've felt judged by others for. But what would happen if instead, we thought of our weird as our superpower? And what if we looked for the beautifully weird superpowers in everybody around us? I invite you to do just that. To seek out differences. To celebrate the weird in yourself and other people.

You've made it to the end of this book. Congrats! Often, when we finish reading a book, we put it back on the shelf or pass it along to a friend and that's that. This time, I invite you to remember the Wheel of Weird and take action. Sometime in the next 24 hours, I invite you to find someone different than you. Someone that you've never had a conversation with before. I invite you to ask them about a time they felt like they didn't belong. Ask them from a mindset of curiosity. Your role in this exercise is not to add comments, not to share your experience. (At least not right now.) It's just to listen to them, and then look them in the eye and say thank you.

And with that... Thank **you** for reading!

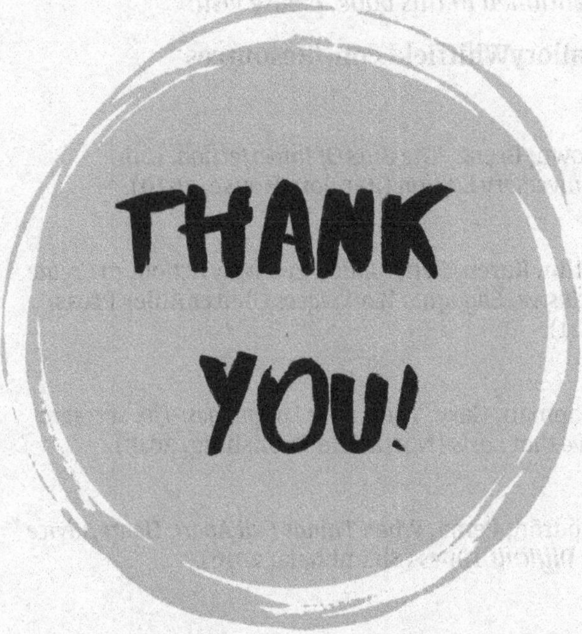
THANK YOU!

References and Recommended Reading

For links to websites and online resources mentioned in this book, please visit:

MalloryWhitfield.com/Resources

Brown, Brené, *The Gifts Of Imperfection, 10th Anniversary Edition* (Random House, 2020).

Catlin, Karen, *Better Allies: Everyday Actions to Create Inclusive, Engaging Workplaces* (Better Allies Press, 2021).

Chapman, Gary, *The 5 Love Languages: The Secret to Love that Lasts* (Northfield Publishing, 2015).

Chödrön, Pema, *When Things Fall Apart: Heart Advice for Difficult Times* (Shambhala, 2016).

Imani, Blair, *Read This to Get Smarter: about Race, Class, Gender, Disability & More* (Ten Speed Press, 2021).

Kimmerer, Robin Wall, *Braiding Sweetgrass: Indigenous Wisdom, Scientific Knowledge and the Teachings of Plants* (Milkweed Editions, 2015).

Loewen, James W, *Lies My Teacher Told Me: Everything Your American History Textbook Got Wrong* (Simon & Schuster, 1995).

Menakem, Resmaa, *My Grandmother's Hands: Racialized Trauma and the Pathway to Mending Our Hearts and Bodies* (Central Recovery Press, 2017).

Neff, Kristin, *Self-Compassion: The Proven Power of Being Kind to Yourself* (William Morrow, 2015).

Rath, Tom, *Strengths Finder 2.0: A New and Upgraded Edition of the Online Test from Gallup's Now, Discover Your Strengths* (Gallup Press, 2007).

Rosenberg, Marshall B, *Nonviolent Communication: A Language of Life* (PuddleDancer Press, 2015).

Ruiz, Don Miguel, *The Four Agreements: A Practical Guide to Personal Freedom* (A Toltec Wisdom Book) (Amber-Allen Publishing, 2018).

Taylor, Sonya Renee, *The Body Is Not an Apology: The Power of Radical Self-Love* (Berrett-Koehler Publishers, 2018).

About the Author

Mallory Whitfield is an artist and keynote speaker with decades of experience speaking and performing on stages of all shapes and sizes. She is also an accomplished entrepreneur and digital marketer. She is the author of *How to Make Money at Craft Shows: Art Market and Craft Fair Tips & Tricks*, which is based on what she learned during 10+ years of selling her handmade clothing and accessories at craft shows. As an Adjunct Professor for Tulane University's School of Professional Advancement, she has taught and developed classes on digital marketing. In 2016, she was named one of *Gambit*'s 40 Under 40, which salutes the brightest innovators, artists, and professionals in New Orleans. Her favorite costume moments include dressing as Cher, David Bowie, and a cassowary, the world's deadliest bird.